A Gift for Saint David's Day

Suzanne Carpenter's illustration for 'Saint David's Day' by Lisa Daniels.

a gift for Saint David's Day

Editor

Neil Nuttall

PONT

To all children everywhere
who celebrate Saint David's Day

Published in 2007 by Pont Books, an imprint of
Gomer Press, Llandysul, Ceredigion SA44 4JL

ISBN 1 84323 679 6
ISBN-13 9781843236795
A CIP record for this title is available from the British Library.

The work of three illustrators is represented in *A Gift for Saint David's Day*.
Brett Breckon illustrated the work on pages 8, 12, 36, 39, 58, 61, 74, 77.
Suzanne Carpenter illustrated the work on pages 2, 30, 32, 51, 54, 71, 91, 93.
Jac Jones illustrated the work on pages 16, 19, 45, 46, 62, 65, 79, 80, 81, 82, 83, 85, 87, 88.

This book is published with the financial support of the
Welsh Books Council.

Printed and bound in Wales at
Gomer Press, Llandysul, Ceredigion

Contents

FOREWORD

For centuries, from the time of Dewi Sant himself, stories have gathered around him, and around St Davids Cathedral, the place where he founded his monastery. Fact and fiction, myth and legend, poetry and drama, all focus on the person of Saint David, on Wales and above all on Tyddewi, that remarkable place hiding in its little valley between land and sea on the western peninsula of Wales. The authors of this miscellany have all been moved to respond in his or her own way to the attraction and inspiration which Dewi Sant and *Gŵyl Ddewi* continue to evoke in the present day.

As Dean of St Davids[1] it therefore gives me great pleasure both to welcome *A Gift for Saint David's Day* and to commend it to your attention.

Wyn Evans
Dean of St Davids

---

[1] Even in English people disagree about the spelling of the various placenames connected with Saint David. You will find all of them at different points in this book: *St David's* or *St Davids, St Non's* or *St Nons, St Justinan* or *St Justinian's*.

Introduction

What's in a name? Dewi Sant or Saint David, Tyddewi or St David's, they are all connected with Wales's patron saint or the places associated with him. We don't know a huge amount about Saint David – or his companions Aidan and Ishmael (Aeddan and Ismael in Welsh) – but we do know a lot about the influence they had on the life of the people of Wales.

In these pages you will find many contributions, in different styles, all of which celebrate the relationship between Saint David and the Welsh people: from Malachy Doyle's retelling of the Saint David legend to Nicola Davies's magical story about Grandpa Noggard.

There are drama scripts: Jenny Sullivan's play-within-a-play, and Ruth Morgan's tale of golden magic. Magic is the theme of the final story where Nain shares the secret of her very special daffodils, whilst our national flower is the subject of Francesca Kay's contribution, and features, too, in Lisa Daniels's poem: Lisa was the winner of our Saint David's Day writing competition for schools.

Suzanne Carpenter prefers the leek to the daffodil, in an entertaining piece about her efforts to learn the Welsh language, whilst Christine Evans and Phil Carradice have written historical stories, one about a novice (trainee) monk, and one about a Viking raid. Nona Rees's fact-filled report about the cathedral at St David's is counterbalanced by Mary Medlicott's intriguing tale about a mysterious stone statue.

Artists Brett Breckon, Suzanne Carpenter and Jac Jones have supplied the gift wrapping to go with each piece of writing and we hope that *A Gift for Saint David's Day* is also a celebration of the writers and illustrators who have honoured him here.

Neil Nuttall
Guest Editor

The Saint, the Druid and the Witch

Malachy Doyle

'*Can we rest for a minute?*'
asked Teilo, struggling to the top
of the hill behind the others.
'*We can do more than rest,*' *replied David,*
admiring the beauty of the land
below him. '*For our journey is at an end.*'

'Is it here that we shall live?' asked Aidan and Ishmael, together.

'Yes,' said David, nodding. 'We shall build huts and a small chapel in this sheltered valley, and it will become our home.'

For many months, David and his followers had been spreading the word of God all through the west of England and south Wales and now they had arrived at Glyn Rhosyn, on the banks of the river Alun.

David wasn't the first outsider to be attracted to the place, though. Some time before, an Irish chieftain named Boia had set up camp just across the valley.

'Look over there,' said Boia to his wife, catching sight of a plume of smoke streaking its way over to them.

'It is fire, husband,' cried Satrapa, narrowing her eyes. 'Someone is trying to steal our land!'

For David was burning grass to clear some ground, and the tradition in those days was that all the land darkened by a settler's smoke would belong to him and him alone.

'Go down, husband,' cried the chieftain's wife. 'Go down and clear them off our property, while you still have the chance!'

But Boia was a druid as well as a chieftain, and he only used violence when he felt there was no other choice. 'I shall speak to them first,' he told his wife. 'It may be possible to live in peace with them.'

'Live in peace!' cried Satrapa, sneering at him. 'Are you a man or a mouse, husband?'

And, not for the first time, Boia wondered whether he had made the right choice in marrying this woman. His first wife had died giving birth to their daughter, Dunod, and Boia had re-married as soon as possible. He had been lonely, so lonely, and the child needed a mother, but Satrapa had turned out to be a difficult woman, prone to terrible rages. And, although he had never actually caught her being cruel to Dunod, Boia sometimes worried that Satrapa did not appear to love his daughter as a mother should.

The chieftain wanted, more than anything though, to recreate the same sort of loving marriage he had with his first wife, and had made a promise to himself never to argue with Satrapa, despite her temper.

In order to keep her happy, therefore, Boia gathered his men around him and marched down the valley. He had hoped that Satrapa would leave him to it, but no – she was determined to go with him.

'You must get rid of these intruders,' she hissed, by his side, 'or I shall do it for you and make you look a fool.'

Boia knew it was important to appear strong. 'Who lit this fire?' he demanded, when they arrived at David's encampment. 'You cannot claim land that is mine!'

'It was my belief that the land here was unclaimed,' the holy man replied, in the gentlest of voices, 'but if I am wrong and it is yours, then I beg of you a small area to build on, for surely there is enough here in this beautiful valley for both of us.'

'There is not!' cried Satrapa. 'We want no nosy neighbours round here!'

David ignored her rudeness and looked into the eyes of the chieftain. 'God has led me to this place,' he told Boia, 'and He is never wrong. I intend to build a monastery here for myself and my companions, but you have nothing to fear, you or your wife, for we are quiet, my people and I. We shall do little but tend our gardens and pray, and we shall not disturb you.'

'We didn't come all the way from Ireland to choose to live next to a bunch of mealy-mouthed Christians, did we, husband?' demanded Satrapa. 'This is our land, all of it,' she cried, turning to David. 'So you'd better go back to where you came from, for you're no match for the mighty Boia and his warriors!'

David was surprised at her anger, but he was not afraid. 'As I told you before, we mean you no harm,' he said, 'but this is Christian land now, and if you will excuse us, it is time for prayer.'

Boia glanced at Satrapa, Satrapa glared in return, and the chieftain knew that if he wanted a quiet life back at home, he had no choice but to do as his wife wished.

'Pray for your lives, then!' he roared, ordering his men to attack. Raising their swords and their spears, they were all for plunging them into the helpless monks, on their knees before them.

'It is you that we shall pray for, not ourselves,' said David in a low voice. He bent his head.

And at that very moment every single one of the soldiers froze, as though turned to ice. Their weapons dropped to the ground, the sound of them clanking on the hard earth broke the spell they were under, and they raced back to camp. 'Help, help!' they cried. 'We've been bewitched!'

'I'll show you bewitched . . .' scowled Satrapa, cursing her husband as they followed on behind. 'You can't even stand up to the power of a monk, Boia! If you're not careful I'll show you the full extent of MY powers one of these days . . .'

And then, as if things weren't bad enough for them, when Boia and Satrapa reached the fields surrounding their camp, they found their oxen and horses lying dead on the ground.

'You speak of powers, woman . . .' whispered the chieftain, stunned at the sight before him. 'But that man's God is a thousand times more powerful than you or me.'

And, while his wife stomped off to plan her revenge, Boia went back to beg the holy man's forgiveness. 'I am deeply sorry for how we treated you,' he said. 'Please tell me about this God of yours.'

Soon he was down on his knees, praying with David and his disciples, and by the time he got home, all of his animals had been brought back to life and were grazing contentedly.

Satrapa, though, was furious when she heard of her husband's conversion. 'Whoever heard of a Christian druid!' she screamed. 'You are a weak and a foolish man, Boia, and it looks like it's going to be up to me to get our land back.'

She sent her maidens to bathe naked in the river Alun, in the hope that David and his monks would be so horrified, or so embarrassed, that they would pack up and leave. But rather than turn his back on them, David, who loved water and often spent all day praying in the river, waded in also, talked to the girls for hours, and ended up baptising more than one.

This, of course, was the final straw for Satrapa. 'I shall do something so horrendous, to them and their God, that it will force those holy men from this land forever!' she hissed.

And the following morning she called to Dunod, her step-daughter. 'Come and gather nuts with me,' she said, and she led the innocent girl down into the valley and deep into the wood.

When they had filled their baskets and come right to the heart of the forest, where Satrapa knew no-one could hear, she said, 'Lay your head in my lap, dear, for I know you must be tired after all your hard work.'

Dunod did as her step-mother suggested, for she had no reason to doubt her, but as soon as she was asleep, Satrapa drew out a knife, as sharp as a warrior's sword, and slit the girl's throat.

When Boia's followers heard what Satrapa had done, for such a wicked deed can never remain secret for long, they went down to David's encampment, pleaded with him to ask his God to protect them from the evil of their mistress, and soon found themselves pledging their lives to the glory of God.

And when Satrapa saw that all her plans were failing and that one by one everyone was deserting her, she rushed to the top of the highest hill, spread her arms to the four winds and proceeded to scream, more loudly than human has ever screamed before.

In response, there was a terrific crash of thunder, a blinding flash of lightning, and when the smoke and the fury had faded from the skies, all that remained on the hilltop, and all that remained of Satrapa, was a smouldering pile of ash.

Poor Boia, having now lost two wives and a much-beloved daughter, took leave of his senses entirely. In the depths of his grief, he came to believe that it was David, not Satrapa, who had been the cause of all his sorrow, and began to plot against him.

Nearly all of his men, though, had by now taken to joining David and his followers down at the monastery for early morning prayers. So that one day, at sunrise, when a bloodthirsty Irish warrior named Lisci landed his boat in the nearest harbour and stormed Boia's camp, there was no-one left to guard him. Lisci lopped off his rival's head, set fire to Boia's settlement and was gone in the blinking of an eye, back to Ireland with his plunder.

And, dreadful though it was, that was the last violent act to take place in the beautiful vale of Glyn Rhosyn. For from that day to this, it has been a haven of peace and Christianity, under the watchful eye of Saint David.

THE DRESS REHEARSAL

Jenny Sullivan

Slow down, Rhodri. Don't gabble!

Characters

Narrator*
Teacher
King Gwrtheyrn
Slave 1
Slave 2
Slave 3
Courtier 1
Courtier 2
Courtier 3
Student Magician Melfyn
Merlin
Guards with spears etc.

* I have given the narrator a name (Rhodri). However, it may add to the play's entertainment value if the narrator uses his/her real name. If possible the class teacher might also play him/herself, and the class year group should be inserted too, where indicated.

The play-within-the-play is my version of an C8th legend.

The scene is the Great Hall of King Gwrtheyrn's Castle.

TEACHER: *[offstage throughout]* Right, class . . . This is absolutely the last rehearsal before Saint David's Day, and this time I want it right, OK? Now concentrate, *everyone*. Right, Rhodri? Off you go. Nice, loud voice now!

NARRATOR: *[facing audience: does not look happy. Muttering]* I think I should have been christened *Rhodri the Blooming Narrator*, that's what I think. That's all I ever get to do, that is. Play the rotten narrator. Do I ever get the chance to dress up? No. *You've got a nice loud voice, Rhodri*, they say. *You can be the narrator, Rhodri*, they say. So everybody else dresses up and I'm stuck in my school uni-

TEACHER: *[warningly]* Rhodri . . .

NARRATOR: Oh, all right, all right. *[Sighs]*
This-is-the-story-of-why-our-flag-shows-a-red-dragon . . .

TEACHER: Slow down, Rhodri. Don't gabble.

NARRATOR: This is the story of why our flag shows a Red Dragon. Once upon a time there was a king named King Gwrtheyrn. He was not a Good King, because he had betrayed his own countrymen in battle, and many of them had been killed. Let's join his courtiers now to find out their opinion of him.

COURTIER 1: *[Courtiers all speak behind their hands, towards audience]* He is incredibly evil!

COURTIER 2: He is amazingly horrible!

COURTIER 3: He is totally wicked and cruel!

SLAVE 1: They think *they've* got problems? At least they aren't slaves, are they? At least he doesn't torture them.

SLAVE 2: And put them in dungeons.

SLAVE 3: And make them work until they drop.

KING: I'm King, I am, and everyone has to do as I say, or else! You there, slave!

SLAVE 1: Who, Sir, me, Sir? Yes, Sir? Master? Your Highness? Sire? Your Majesty? Your, Your, um – Your Terribleness?

KING: Fetch me some strawberries, now, slave! Fresh, ripe, red, juicy ones. AND some ice cream! And don't forget to grovel while you're doing it!

SLAVE 2: But, Your Magnificentness, strawberries aren't in season! There aren't any strawberries at all, not in March! And nobody's invented ice cream yet!

KING: That's no excuse! Guards! Throw them in the dungeons! Torture them until they bring me my strawberries! And you! Courtier Number Two! Invent me some ice cream! Now!

Slaves 1 and 2 are dragged offstage, struggling, by the guards, who then return. The other slaves shake their heads, sadly. Courtier Number Two scratches his head, looks puzzled, and wanders off after them.

KING: One is King, and One has decided that One is going to build Oneself a nice new castle.

COURTIER 1: A new castle, One's Majesty? May one ask where?

KING: One may. One is – oh, phooey. *I'm* going to build it right on top of that hill out there. So I can look down at my old castle and remember how rich I am.

Courtier Two returns. He is carrying a large bowl marked 'ice cream'. He dips a wooden spoon into the (runny) mixture, looks into the bowl and shakes his head sadly. He glances at the King and hides the bowl.

COURTIER 3: I'm sure it will be a very fine castle, Your Majesty.

KING: Of course it will! It will be the finest castle in all Wales. Because *I* am going to build it! *I! Me! One!* And it will be mine, all mine. Ha-ha-ha-ha ha-ha-ha-ha-haaaaah!

COURTIER 1: *[behind hand, to audience]* Oh dear. He's having one of his not very funny turns again!

NARRATOR: At least he gets to *dress up* and have funny turns. Do I ever get to dress up? No, I don't. Not ever. It's always, *Rhodri, you can be the narrator.* I ask you, is that fair? Is it?

TEACHER: Rhodri! Stop sulking and get on with it!

At this point, the missing slaves return.

NARRATOR: *[loudly]* Oh, all right. *[More quietly but still audibly]* Don't get your underwear in an uproar. What happens next? Oh yes. So anyway, the King set his slaves to build his fine new castle on the hill. On the first day the slaves had to remove a huge rock that was blocking their way, so that they could haul all the stones and stuff up the hill to build the castle.

SLAVE 1: We worked all day, we did, from sunrise –

SLAVE 2:   – to sunset. Exhausting, it was! My back was killing me! And oh! how my feet hurt!

SLAVE 3:   Any normal Master would have let us have a lunch break, and maybe even coffee breaks, but not King Gwrtheyrn, oh no, not him.

SLAVE 1:   We worked until it was too dark to see any more, and the foundations of the new castle were laid, and –

SLAVE 2:   – and the walls of the new castle were just beginning to rise on the hill. Looked a treat, it did.

SLAVE 3:   When we couldn't see what we were doing any more, he let us go home to bed. If you could call it bed.

SLAVE 1:   It was just a hard floor. No blankets. But he did give us some supper.

SLAVE 2:   If you could call it supper.

SLAVE 3:   It was leftovers from his own dinner.

SLAVE 1:   But he was very kind. *[Sarcastically]* I mean, he even chewed some of the food for us, first! The gristly, fatty, yukky bits.

KING: Are you lot complaining? I could arrange for you to starve, you know!

NARRATOR: He's totally horrible, isn't he? Like, really, really nasty. And STILL he gets a chance to dress up!

TEACHER: Rhodri! If I've told you once –

NARRATOR: I know, I know. Where was I? Oh, yes. Well, next morning, the King woke up and looked out of his window, expecting to see the slaves hard at work on his new castle. He stared. He could hardly believe his eyes. His castle had disappeared completely, and where the foundations and walls had been the day before, there was nothing but smooth, green grass. His slaves stood around scratching their heads and looking puzzled.

KING: Where is it? Who's got it? Who's pinched my lovely new castle? *[Glares at courtiers]* Was it you? Are you trying to be funny? Because if you are, I've got some nice cold, damp dungeons downstairs, and a very under-employed torturer!

COURTIERS: *[together, quaking]* No, Your Majesty! We're just as surprised as you are, Your Majesty. Please don't send us to the dungeons!

KING: Then come up with some ideas! Don't just stand there! Find out who did it, why don't you? Go on, think of something!

COURTIER 1: Well, Your Majesty, you could try sending for Your Magician. Perhaps he'll know.

KING: My Magician? Have I got one? Oh, yes. So I have. Right. Send for my Magician!

COURTIER 3: *[behind hand, to audience]* He might as well not have a Magician for all the good this one is. He's only a little lad. He's failed his Grade One exams three times so far, and he certainly hasn't earned his pointy hat yet! He doesn't get that until he passes Grade Ten!

COURTIER 1: Fetch the Magician! Where's the Magician?

The Magician enters. He is very nervous and very scruffy, with large spectacles and a large, floppy flat hat that keeps falling over his nose.

KING: *[in tones of disgust]* Are *you* my Magician? Good grief!

MAGICIAN: Yes, Sire. I mean, Your Majesty. Your Terribleness. Your Highness. Your, Your, Your Splendiferousness! I am. It's me. Your Magician, Your Remarkable Worshipfulness.

KING: That'll do, that'll do. Don't get carried away. I know how Magnificent I am and all that. *[Peers at Magician]* You look familiar. Do I know you? What's your name? Begins with a P? Perkins? Peebles? Peregrine? Porter? Something like that?

MAGICIAN: N-n-no, Your Highness. It's Merfyn, actually. You hired me last year.

KING: Did I? Oh, well. I hope I don't pay you too much.

MAGICIAN: No, Your Majesty. You haven't paid me anything at all yet.

KING: Good. Now, Magician, earn your pay – if I ever decide to give you any. Tell me – what's happened to my magnificent new castle? Where's it gone?

MAGICIAN: *[terrified]* I don't kn-n-now, Your Majesty. There's really only one Magician powerful enough to know things like that, Your Majesty, and that's not me. It's the one and only Great Merlin, Y-your Majesty.

KING:	Merlin? Never heard of him. Send for him! Now! At once! Immediately! I want him here *yesterday*. If not sooner!
NARRATOR:	Now, as I expect you know, no-one *sends for* Merlin. Merlin comes *when* and *if* he wants to, or not at all. But it just so happened that Merlin had intended to visit evil King Gwrtheyrn all along. So he put on his robe and his pointy hat (see, *he* got a chance to dress up, didn't he? No-one made HIM be the narrator, did they?).
TEACHER:	*[warningly]* Rhodr*iii*!
NARRATOR:	Yes, miss, all right, I heard you. I know, get on with it, Rhodri. Anyway, Merlin arrived, probably in a puff of smoke, with thunderclaps and stuff like that, but you'll have to imagine that bit, all right? Who do you think I am, Steven Spielberg?
MERLIN:	*[disbelievingly]* You – ah – *sent* for me, I believe.
KING:	*[frowning]* You sent for me, *Your Majesty!*
MERLIN:	You don't need to call me 'Your Majesty'. 'Great Merlin' will do. And I didn't send for you. You sent for me. And *I* decided to come. So. What do you want?
KING:	I demand to know who has taken my castle! I was building it on that hill over there, and this morning it's all gone. Disappeared!
SLAVE 1:	*He* was building it? I like that!
MERLIN:	*[stroking his beard and looking thoughtful]* You *demand*, do you? I see. Well, King Gwrtheyrn, I must tell you that it would be best if you built your castle somewhere else.

24

NARRATOR: As you can imagine, this did not please the King at all: he was not a Happy Bunny. In fact, he was furious!

KING: You what? How dare you? If I want to build my castle on top of that hill, I shall build my castle there, and nobody's going to stop me!

NARRATOR: Want to bet?

TEACHER: That isn't in the script, Rhodri.

MERLIN: Yesterday, you made your slaves move a huge rock from the bottom of the hill. Two or three of them got squashed, and several broke arms and legs, and some pulled muscles, but you didn't care, did you? Anyway, where that rock was, there is now a vast lake, which is deeper than you can imagine. The answer to your problems lies at the bottom of that lake. Which is, of course, full of water. And unless you get to the root of the problem, you will never build your castle. The root of your problem is, as I said, at the bottom of the lake.

KING: Then I shall empty it!

SLAVE 2: He means, *we* shall empty it, of course. We shan't see *him* outside paddling around with his trouser legs rolled up, carrying a bucket, shall we? Oh, no. It'll be –

KING: Get on with it, you lot, or it's dungeons and torture for you.

SLAVE 1: And whips and chains and red hot irons and stuff, too, I expect. Honestly, it's so jolly unfair. And I bet there won't be any coffee breaks!

KING: The only breaks you'll get are the sort that are set in plaster! I said, get on with it, if you know what's good for you!

NARRATOR: So the slaves, who *did* know what was good for them, set to with their buckets and worked from sunrise to sunset, and then by the light of flaming torches, far into the night until the lake was emptied. When at last it was dry, at the very bottom of the lake they discovered two vast, sleeping dragons: one that was as white as snow, and one that was as red as fire.

KING: Dragons. Well, goodness me. Tomorrow, when it's light, I'll get my guards to chase them away. Or maybe my slaves. They're cheaper.

NARRATOR: Dawn came, and the sun rose. As soon as the last drop of water had dried on the dragons' scales, they woke up and began to fight. They fought ferociously all day, and at sunset, the white dragon lay vanquished and dead on the dry bed of the lake. The red dragon had won the battle. It was a bit like Wales and England in the final of the Six Nations, really.

TEACHER: Thank you, Rhodri. That isn't in the script, either.

MERLIN: There. The White Dragon is dead. The battle is over.

KING: No, it isn't, you stupid man! How can the battle be over when there's still a dragon left to kill?

NARRATOR: Then, Merlin got really, really angry . . . No-one calls Merlin stupid!

MERLIN: *[looking furious]* King Gwrtheyrn, listen to me, and listen carefully. The dragon that has been killed was a magical

symbol of your own terrible cowardice. It stands for your dreadful behaviour. You betrayed your own people to the enemy, which is the worst thing any King can do. You don't deserve to be King. Let the White Dragon's death be a terrible warning to you.

KING: I don't believe a word of it! Who do you think you are, coming here handing out warnings! How dare you?

MERLIN: I dare, King Gwrtheyrn, because I am the Great Merlin of Wales. And I am here to warn you that if you don't go away, right now, and never come back, the Red Dragon will kill you, just as it killed the White Dragon. There is no room in Wales for traitors and cowards. Run away, Gwrtheyrn, while you still have legs to run . . .

KING: Oh. Well, if you're going to put it like that . . . The Red Dragon will kill me, you say?

MERLIN: It will chomp you into chump chops and barbecue the bits.

KING: That sounds quite a permanent kind of killing, to me. And sort of painful, too. I don't like pain, unless it's other people's. Maybe you're right. I – um – perhaps I *should* take a bit of a holiday. A LONG holiday. A long, long holiday far, far away from here. *[Sighs]* The neighbourhood's gone downhill anyway. Magicians and Dragons move in, and all the nice personages move out.

COURTIER 1:   What idiot told him he was a nice personage?

KING: Don't get too clever, Number One – I haven't gone yet! Slaves!

SLAVES: *[together]* Yes, Your Majesty?

KING: Pack my suitcase.

SLAVE 1:   With pleasure, Your Majesty. *[Behind his hand to audience]* His mother didn't teach him to say 'please', either, did she?

                  A suitcase is brought and the King, slinking, exits, cheered loudly by his waving slaves and courtiers. The suitcase has a large destination sticker. This should be chosen for local effect!

NARRATOR: When the horrible, evil, cruel, cowardly King ~

KING: *[offstage]* I heard that!

NARRATOR: So what? You aren't in the play any more! As I was saying, when the horrible, evil, cruel, cowardly, wicked and very rude and ill-mannered King had gone, Merlin built himself a fortress exactly where the King had planned to build his own. He called it Caer Fyrddin – Merlin's Fortress – which is now known to us as Carmarthen.

                  And from that day onward, the Welsh flag has always shown a fiery Red Dragon on a green and white field.

                  Slaves 1 and 2 enter, bearing the Welsh flag outstretched. They creep up behind the narrator *and drape it over his head and round his shoulders like a cloak.*

TEACHER: *[laughing]* There you are, Rhodri! You got dressed up after all! Well done, Year . . . That was a really good rehearsal!

Heralds of Spring

Francesca Kay

Long ago, a Herald was a person who told everyone what was going on. He delivered important messages, and made announcements, and did it in a very loud voice, so nobody missed a thing.

Our own daffodil, one of the emblems of Wales, is also a herald. It tells us that spring is here, and summer is on its way. Of course, daffodils don't have loud voices, but they are bright and beautiful. When they start to bloom, we know that the winter will soon be over.

The daffodil comes from a bulb. It looks a little like an onion (although you shouldn't eat daffodil bulbs, as they are poisonous!) and it's planted deep in the soil. It starts to send up leaves and flower buds as the winter ends. There's one type of this flower that only grows in Tenby – it might be the original Welsh daffodil. You can see carpets of daffodils planted all along the roadsides in Wales, and in parks and gardens too, and they grow up every year.

On Saint David's Day we proudly wear a daffodil as a symbol of Wales. It's one of the ways we celebrate our saint's day. Another plant we wear on this day is the leek. Very different, you might think, but their names in Welsh are the same! The Welsh word for leek is *cenhinen*, and the Welsh word for daffodil is *cenhinen Bedr.* So it's a little confusing when you're writing about daffodils and leeks, but who would mix up a muddy green vegetable with a marvellous yellow flower?

Here's some Latin now. The Latin name for daffodil is *narcissus.* There's a Greek legend that tells of a handsome but heartless boy named Narcissus. A lovely nymph called Echo fell desperately in love with him. Echo could not talk in her own words, however. She could only repeat someone else's. Narcissus was lost in the woods one day, and Echo was following him. He called out, 'Is anyone here?' All that Echo could reply was, 'Here, here, here.' Narcissus mocked her for repeating everything he said, and sent her away. With her heart broken, Echo hid, and slowly faded until only her voice was left. Narcissus was punished for his cruelty by the gods, who made him fall in love with his own reflection. He sat down by a pond, gazing at himself in the water. He was there for so long that he too faded into a beautiful nodding flower, the *narcissus.*

Daffodils really do seem to nod and dance when the breeze blows. William Wordsworth, a very famous poet, wrote a poem about daffodils. It is one of the best known poems ever written. Here is the first verse. Have you heard it before?

> I wandered lonely as a cloud,
> That floats on high o'er vales and hills,
> When all at once I saw a crowd,
> A host of golden daffodils,
> Beside the lake, beneath the trees,
> Fluttering and dancing in the breeze.

Wordsworth wasn't in Wales when he saw the flowers that inspired this poem, but he could have been writing about our own lovely displays of daffodils.

Daffodils come in many shades of that happy colour yellow. Have you ever tried drawing one? It's really quite difficult because of its interesting shape. There's a long straight stem, and then the petals are arranged around a trumpet. That's the middle of the flower. Not many flowers have a trumpet!

Those Heralds of years gone by would often blow a trumpet to grab everyone's attention before telling them what they needed to know. Imagine if daffodils could make a real trumpet sound. What a bright and cheerful noise it would be. Our gardens would be very noisy places for a while in the early spring! Perhaps it would be a good idea if we all wrote poems instead!

Heralds of Change

A splash of cold as
The sharp spring rain is falling,
And Nature wakes up.

Stout stems and long leaves,
They move in the harsh spring wind,
The new season comes.

Look at these flowers,
Glowing in the pale spring sun,
Winter creeps away.

Bright trumpets pointing
Through spring to summer glory,
The world is turning.

The verses in this poem are written in haiku form. The first line of each verse has 5 syllables, the second has 7 syllables, and the third 5 syllables again. Perhaps you could try a poem with a pattern like this one.

The poem has another pattern too. Can you find it? (The answer is on page 96).

How to plant daffodils – and keep them happy!

- Plant your daffodil bulbs from August to November.

- Plant them nice and deep. Try and plant them at a depth that's about three times the height of the bulb – or even a little deeper. This will make them happy and they will flower for you every year!

- When your daffodils have finished flowering, take off the dead flower heads, and then, when the leaves have gone all yellow and floppy, cut them off and wait. They'll be back next spring!

- Daffodils look good in pots on your patio, or in the garden border, or even planted in the grass. If you have lots in your garden, then you can pick some to arrange in a vase indoors.

Saint David and his Cathedral

Nona Rees

If you come to Tyddewi or St Davids today, you will see many things that have not changed for hundreds of years.

The beaches, rocky cliffs and islands are the same ones that Saint David would have seen. There is a ruined chapel on a cliff top which marks where he was born, and a holy well nearby. The place is called St Nons, after his mother.

David was baptised at the top of Porth Clais harbour where there was another little chapel and holy well that have now disappeared. Clegyr Boia, the Iron Age fort of the chieftain Boia who tried to stop David coming to the valley, overlooks Glyn Rhosyn (valley of the little marsh).

This is where David, Teilo, Ismael and Aeddan built the first simple stone and turf huts, thatched with reeds. One of the buildings would have been a little chapel called an *oratory*. Saint David and his companions would be very surprised to see a great cathedral there today.

The sort of life they lived seems very hard to us. The day would start at sunrise and end late at night with prayers. In between, the monks worked in the fields, pulling ploughs yoked to their shoulders. They also looked after people who were sick or poor. All year round, they wore tunics of animal skins with perhaps a rough woven cloak and sandals on their feet. They ate mainly vegetables such as roots and watercress, perhaps coarse, stone-ground bread and, in David's monastery, had only water to drink. The monks would have spoken an early type of Welsh, also Irish and Latin. David is sometimes known as the Waterman, *Dewi Dyfrwr*, because, as a penance, he would stand up to his neck in cold water and recite the Psalms.

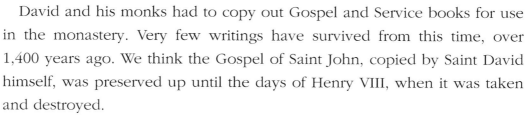

David and his monks had to copy out Gospel and Service books for use in the monastery. Very few writings have survived from this time, over 1,400 years ago. We think the Gospel of Saint John, copied by Saint David himself, was preserved up until the days of Henry VIII, when it was taken and destroyed.

David travelled widely during his lifetime. When he was young, there was a deadly illness called jaundice which turned people yellow. It was called the Yellow Plague and most people who caught it died from it. Because of this disease, David and his mother, Non, with many others, escaped to Brittany until it was safe to return. Many places in Brittany are dedicated to Saint David and Saint Non. David travelled all over south Wales and founded many churches. He established some in England too and went on pilgrimage to Jerusalem with Saint Teilo and Saint Padarn. He preached to the churchmen of Wales at Llanddewi Brefi. People had difficulty in seeing him but his sermon was so good that the ground rose up under him, a white dove flew onto his shoulder and David was made chief of all the bishops.

David lived to be a very old man; he was born in the early years of the sixth century and died towards the end of the century. The place was not called St Davids until hundreds of years after his death. It was known as *Mynyw*, which means a grove of small trees and bushes. Later on this was translated into Latin and called *Menevia*.

After David's time, life in the Valley changed dramatically. The next few hundred years are known as the Dark Ages because we know so little about them. In Wales, law and order broke down and there was much fighting among the different tribes. Angles and Saxons invaded from the east but an even more deadly threat came from the sea. The whole coast of Wales suffered from fierce Viking raids. These men from the north sailed round the coast of Wales in longboats. They plundered the little monastery, took anything of value and set fire to all the rest. The people of St Davids had dark memories of these times, when even two bishops, Morgeneu and Abraham, were killed.

Eventually the place was almost deserted and people forgot where Saint David was buried. His grave became so overgrown that it took a priest seven days to hack his way through brambles to find it. The only things that remain from this time are a few beautifully carved stones in memory of people who died. They are called cross-inscribed stones and you can see them today in a cathedral exhibition.

After the Vikings, a very different invasion took place, one that was to change Britain for ever. William the Conqueror arrived in 1066 and, with his Norman army, conquered the whole country in the Battle of Hastings. The king came to St Davids on pilgrimage in 1081. It was very important to go on pilgrimage to pray at the shrine or burial place of a saint. If you did this, it was believed that your sins would be forgiven and illnesses would be cured. In 1123, Pope Callistus II told people that two pilgrimages to St Davids were as good as going all the way to Rome. Thousands of people must have come to St Davids and in 1131 the first cathedral was built, fifty years after the first biography (life story) of Saint David was written. The scribe's name was Rhygyfarch and he tells us that he wrote it using all the ancient books he could find in the monastery, even though they were crumbling with age and eaten away by worms. We owe most of what we know about Saint David to Rhygyfarch.

The next royal visitor was King Henry II, who came on pilgrimage in 1172 to ask forgiveness for the murder of Thomas Becket, Archbishop of Canterbury. He landed at the harbour of St Justinan two miles from the cathedral and walked barefoot all the way. Not long after this visit, Bishop Peter de Leia knocked down the first cathedral and, in 1181, built the one we have today. We do not know what the earlier buildings looked like.

In the middle of the thirteenth century, everyone got very excited because, at last, the grave of Saint David had been discovered. King

PORTH CLAIS

ST JUSTINIAN'S

CLEGYR BOIA

ST NON'S

ST DAVID'S

Edward I gave money towards a special tomb called a shrine, built inside the cathedral, and in 1284 he came to St Davids with Queen Eleanor. You can still see that shrine today.

The next big change was to bring hard times to the cathedral. This was in 1535, when Henry VIII declared that he was head of the church and not the Pope in Rome. People were forbidden to go on pilgrimage and the relics of saints, beautiful shrines, statues, paintings and holy wells were destroyed. Worse was to follow with the Civil War in the 1640s. Oliver Cromwell's troops rode into the cathedral on their horses; they stripped the lead off the roof at the east end to make musket balls. They tried to get the bells out of the tower and broke up any statues that might have survived from King Henry's time. They did so much damage that, by the eighteenth century, part of the cathedral was roofless and the west end was leaning dangerously, ready to collapse. We are lucky to have this ancient cathedral today.

The cathedral was saved in two ways: first, in 1856 an important book was published describing the building and the state it was in: *The History and Antiquities of St Davids*, by W B Jones and E A Freeman. This made people realize what they were about to lose. Sir Gilbert Scott, a very clever architect, then saved the building, beginning his work in 1865. The tower was nearly falling down and the first thing he did was to mend a huge crack in it, made by Cromwell's men. He did this by draining streams of water from two wells, which were running under the cathedral, pouring cement into the foundations and putting special rods called tie rods into the tower to strengthen it.

In 1956, the royal visitors came back. Queen Elizabeth II and Prince Philip attended a service. Since then the Queen has paid three more visits: in 1982 she gave out the Royal Maundy Money and in 1995 she presented St Davids with the City Charter. St Davids is not a town or a village; it is a city because it has a cathedral, the 'seat' or throne of a bishop. You can see the Welsh word '*cadair*' (chair) in the title '*eglwys* gadeir*iol*' (cathedral church). The Queen has her own special seat or *stall* in the *quire* that she uses each time she visits. It has the Royal Coat of Arms above it.

Almost everything you see when you come into the cathedral is at least 500 years old. Some of it is much older. You will notice the slope of the floor and the way the pillars lean slightly outwards. This is because the building is on soft marshy ground and has tilted over hundreds of years. Above the *nave* is a fine oak ceiling carved with dolphins and strange faces. The bishop's great carved throne is in the *quire* and round each side are wooden seats for the clergy. These are called *misericords* and underneath there are carvings of people, animals, boats, monsters and scenes from the Middle Ages. There are also carved stone tombs of bishops, priests and knights. You can still see statues in the cathedral, including two of Saint David. The statues and the stained glass are all twentieth-century. Beyond the *quire* is an area called the *presbytery*. Here you can see the medieval shrine of Saint David, the tomb of Edmund Tudor (grandfather of Henry VIII) and above the High Altar, in gold and coloured mosaic, there are two scenes from the life of Saint David. There is so much to see that the best thing to do is to come and visit.

On the day Saint David died, it is said that the whole place was filled with angels and his last words have a message for everyone:

'Brothers and sisters, be cheerful and keep your faith and belief, and do the little things that you have seen and heard through me.'

Owain and the Dragon

Phil Carradice

Along, long time ago in Wales when there were birds the size of elephants – well, perhaps not elephants, say birds the size of sheep or goats – the country was a wild and windswept place. Owain lived with his mother in a cottage on the coast.

It was a hard life. The wind cut across the headland, sharp as a million arrowheads. Winter or summer, it always seemed to be blowing.

It rained as well, hard driving rain, and Owain always felt wet. The rain forced its way into his bed so that he woke in the morning on damp straw, and he tended to the crops or watched over the village goats with the rain always running down his neck. He went to sleep each night with his hair damp and his feet wet.

'I'm fed up with always being wet and cold,' he complained one morning.

His friend Carys looked at him and shook her head. They were out on the headland and were supposed to be scaring birds off the villagers' fields. In fact, all they were doing was hiding behind the stone boundary wall, sheltering from the constant rain. It was the first day of March, almost the end of winter, but nobody would have guessed.

'Never mind the rain,' said Carys. 'Try worrying about the Dragon instead. He's much more trouble than a bit of rain, especially if he decides to come today.'

'Maybe Saint David will protect us!' snorted Owain. He sneered and threw a stone at one of the black crows that hovered, almost motionless in the wind, above their heads. The bird glared at him with its yellow eyes but did not attempt to fly away.

Owain did not believe in Saint David. He did not believe the man had ever existed and he certainly did not believe in his ability to protect the villagers. If the saint had any power at all, he would have stopped the wind and the rain, Owain thought. And he would certainly have protected them all from the Dragon.

The Dragon had been raiding the coast for several years now. Everyone in the village was terrified of him, frightened that one day he and his followers would appear out of the mist, burning and killing anyone who crossed their path. Owain had never seen him. In fact he did not know anyone who'd ever laid eyes on him but everyone said he was ten feet tall and breathed out smoke and fire from his mouth and nostrils.

Owain and Carys sat silently behind the wall. The day dragged on and soon Owain's head fell forward onto his chest. Despite the cold he was fast asleep.

The next thing he knew, Carys was shaking him by the shoulder, pushing and forcing him back into wakefulness.

'Owain, Owain!' she whispered. 'Look, it's the Dragon.'

With fear clawing at his heart, Owain crawled to his knees and stared over the top of the low wall. He gasped. Barely a hundred paces away stood a sight he had hoped never to see. The Dragon's enormous head was scarred and scaly while long streaks of fire seemed to be curling like seaweed across his jaws. His powerful arms and legs were sheathed in a silver metal. Behind him stood twenty or thirty warriors, all dressed in armour and all carrying long swords or battleaxes in their hands.

'What shall we do?' said Carys.

Owain dropped back behind the wall and began to think. They couldn't deal with this alone; they had to get help.

'You go back to the village,' he ordered. 'Warn them all. Send some of the men up here. And, Carys, tell them to bring their pitchforks.'

Carys nodded. 'Take this,' she said. 'Just in case.' In her palm lay a perfectly round, smooth pebble. She slipped it into Owain's hand.

'Hurry, Carys!' he said.

Bending low, she sped off in the direction of the village. Owain sat with his back against the wall and waited. Every so often he would peep over the top to make sure the Dragon and his followers had not gone. They were still there, sitting or standing around a huge fire they had built for themselves.

What are they waiting for? Owain wondered.

Suddenly, he was conscious of another presence. He didn't see anyone approach, just felt that he was no longer alone. He spun around and there, in a low dip in the ground, barely ten feet away, stood an old man. He wore a braided robe and had a long white beard. As Owain opened his mouth to shout, the old man raised a finger to his lips and slowly shook his head. Immediately, a strange feeling of safety and security came over Owain. His mouth closed.

'What are you hiding from?' asked the man in a soft voice.

'The Dragon,' said Owain. He gestured across the wall.

The old man walked to Owain's side and stared. 'There's no dragon.'

'There!' said Owain, pointing. 'There! Can't you see him?'

The old man glanced at the boy and smiled. 'I see men. I don't see a dragon.'

'The big one,' Owain whispered urgently, 'the big one standing at the fire with flames around his head and metal on his arms.'

The old man smiled again. 'I see no dragon.'

Owain paused and stared into space.

'You're afraid. Don't be,' said the old man. 'Trust me. Have courage. There is no dragon.'

Once more Owain felt the smoothness of the pebble in his hand. He looked back at the Dragon and gripped the pebble tight. Suddenly he drew back his arm and threw. The missile arced across the headland and struck the Dragon on the side of his head. There was a hollow thud. The Dragon and all his warriors spun around in surprise. For a moment no-one moved and then the Dragon reached up and slowly, carefully, pulled off his head.

Owain gasped. 'It's a man!' he stuttered. 'A man in a mask. He's not a dragon at all.'

The old man nodded. 'A Norseman, a Viking raider, that's all. A tall one, I must admit, but he's no dragon, Owain. It's a trick.'

From behind them came a loud roar. Owain turned. The villagers, Carys amongst them, were lining the bank behind the wall. There must have been thirty of them and they were all armed with pitchforks and scythes. More importantly, they had all seen the Dragon take off his head.

'It's not a dragon,' someone shouted. 'It's only a man dressed up.'

All fear had gone in an instant and the villagers charged. They leapt across the wall and, before the startled Norsemen knew what was happening, they were on them. The battle was short and sharp. In two minutes the raiders were running for their ship in the bay below. Soon, all that was left behind was the occasional shield, the odd sword here and there and, alongside the fire, a battered helmet in the shape of a dragon's head.

'How did you know?' asked Owain, turning back towards the old man. 'How did you guess?'

The old man shrugged. 'Wisdom comes to those who want it, Owain. Fear masks wisdom. Remember, the only thing to really fear is fear itself.'

'Who are you?' Owain said.

The old man reached out and gently ruffled Owain's hair. 'Today is my special day. You should know me by that.'

In the distance Owain heard Carys panting up the hillside towards them. She was breathless and excited. 'Did you see it?' she called. 'Did you see them beat the Dragon?'

Owain shook his head and leaned casually on the wall.

'No, not a dragon, Carys, just a man dressed up. Come here – there's someone I want you to meet.'

He caught her arm and pulled her towards him. But when he turned around, the old man had gone, as silently and as mysteriously as he had come.

'Who?' Carys demanded. 'Who did you want me to meet? There's no-one here. Sometimes, Owain, you are so strange. Come on, the men are putting the Dragon's head onto the fire. Let's go and see it burn.' She spun around and tore off down the slope.

Owain stood, deep in thought. 'Thank you, Saint David,' he whispered at last. 'Thank you for your help, for showing me the way.'

And then he leapt easily over the wall and ran down the hill to where the Dragon's head was already starting to breathe out fire and smoke, blistering and burning in the dancing flames.

Lost for Words

Suzanne Carpenter

W*hen the phone rang*
I was alone in my office and I was very,
very busy. I was very busy ripping up paper
and sticking it back together again and I was
very busy practising speaking Welsh.

I've had lots of Welsh lessons and I've been doing quite well . . . when I'm talking to myself. But, you see, I've got a bit of a problem. If anyone else is in the room, *dw i ddim yn gallu siarad Cymraeg o gwbl*! (I can't speak Welsh at all.) And I mean ANYONE. Even if they're the nicest, kindest, most patient person in Wales (and I know someone who is), my brain turns to playdough and all my Welsh words jumble together and get stuck in it. My eyebrows knit together, I gape like a fish and I can only find two sounds – um, um. It's a problem all right. Still, I'm not going to give up. 'Practice makes perfect,' that's what I say.

Anyway, when the phone rang and Mrs Taclus, the headteacher of Abertwt school, asked me to visit on 1 March to work with the children, I was delighted. What could be nicer than being invited into school on Saint David's Day? Daffodils and dragons, poems and pictures, stories and songs, Welsh cakes and costumes. I was just drifting off into a Saint David's Day daydream when I heard Mrs Taclus say, 'When we heard you'd been learning to speak Welsh we thought you'd be the perfect guest on our day of celebration. The children in the Welsh language unit are already looking forward to meeting you.'

'Um . . . um . . . um.'

Either my stomach was doing somersaults or I had accidentally swallowed a fly. That can happen if you're gaping!

Well what could I do? You can't tell a headteacher that you're scared speechless. Can you? Well I didn't.

'*Hyfryd,*' (Lovely) I replied. 'I'm really looking forward to meeting you all.' And then I went to put the kettle on. At least I'd managed to squeeze out one Welsh word. Maybe things were improving.

'*Dewi Sant, Dewi Sant, Dewi Sant,*' I practised as I poured the tea. Now I know the stories say that Saint David lived on bread, leeks and water (*bara*, *cennin* and *dŵr*). In fact he was known as *Dewi Dyfrwr*, Dewi the waterdrinker. But can you believe it? I mean I know water is really, really good for you, but imagine how fed up you'd feel. No orange juice or milky morning coffee, no fizzy pop or afternoon tea. Not a splash of squash, a sip of soda nor a slurp of slushpuppy. I wonder what he did on his birthday. Did he put candles in his bread and play pass-the-leeky-parcel? Did he decorate his water with a cocktail stick umbrella and a plastic dragon? Probably not. I expect he was too busy helping to feed, clothe and shelter the poor and the needy. Dewi Sant believed in hard work. I expect he'd be impressed with me. As I said, I'm a very busy person.

An hour and three cups of tea later, it was nearly time to have lunch. I had been very busy staring out of the window. To some people it may have looked as if I wasn't doing anything. But, I know that you know that staring out of the window is a very important business. I had been thinking very hard, and do you want to know what I thought? I'll tell you anyway – I thought Dewi Sant sounded a bit grumpy. He only ate bread and leeks – that's enough to make anyone moody. He felt that monks should lead a hard life. And he didn't believe in putting animals to work, oh no. So his followers had to get up at dawn and pull heavy awkward ploughs through the lumpy, bumpy earth. He also said that they should be silent – except when they were saying their prayers or, perhaps, in an emergency. Probably because he didn't want to hear them complaining!

Maybe, if he'd had a balanced diet and a little more rest, he would have been a bit jollier, I thought.

Two pieces of toast, a tomato, a chunk of cheese, a banana, an apple and a chocolate biscuit later, it was nearly time to put the kettle on again. And all that while I was busy thinking about trying to speak Welsh to a class of cheerful children with bright young brains like yours. Me, Mrs Dough Brain, standing at the front, impersonating an um-ing goldfish.

Usually, being an illustrator, I work all alone in my office and I've only got myself to talk to. I always know what I'm going to say next, so there aren't many surprises. Well it's not like that with children, as you know. Your brains are bright, and they're bouncy.

Last year on Saint David's Day I visited a school. I was about to make some pictures with a group of children and I said, 'Saint David is often seen with a white dove on his shoulder. It's a symbol of the Holy Spirit.'

And someone said, 'When I've got a holey sock, my mum says, *You've got a spud in your sock.*'

And someone else said, 'My dad says spuds will grow in your ears if you don't wash them.'

And someone else said, 'My grampy grows spuds and he's got a dovecote and a chicken coop on his allotment.'

And someone else said, 'My nan and gramps have got twelve rabbits, two donkeys and a dalmation.'

And someone else said, 'I've got *101 Dalmations* on DVD and I've watched it 101 times.'

So we'd bounced from Dewi to Dalmations. I tried to imagine having the same conversation in Welsh. I felt that fly in my stomach charging around again!

Oh well, I've heard that when Saint David went to preach at Llanddewi Brefi, the ground beneath his feet rose up so that the crowds could hear him speak. Maybe if I get stuck for words, the ground beneath my feet will open up and swallow me. What a relief that would be, but I don't hold out much hope. Unlike Saint David, I haven't had a lot of success working miracles. Unless you count making pictures out of ripped paper and scribble, of course.

I boiled the kettle for another cup of tea. As I watched the steam billowing, I imagined Dewi looking down from a fluffy white cloudy heaven. Maybe if I said a little prayer and reminded him of past miracles,

he might consider helping me. I mean Saint Elvis of Munster was completely blind until he had the good fortune to baptise Dewi. A few drops of water from the font splashed onto his face and, in the blink of an eye, he could see. Imagine if Dewi could sprinkle a few drops of rain from his cloud onto me. I could catch them on the end of my tongue and – *Hey Presto!* – lots of lovely Welsh words would spring right off the end of it.

Oh, I know it was just a daydream but it would be nice, wouldn't it? Because you know what the alternative is, don't you? Yes, that's right, I'd have to manage on my own. Practice makes perfect, so I'm going to be very, very busy indeed.

I'd better get a move on, I thought, it'll be dinner time soon. I sat at my desk and stared at the mountain of ripped paper I'd created earlier. My dictionary (*geiriadur)* was there somewhere, I was sure of it. Right, I thought, if I can just memorise every word in it *bydd popeth yn iawn* – everything will be all right.

. . . Do you ever feel as if your memory has a leak in it?

Abergofiant (forgetfulness), is the thirteenth word in my Welsh dictionary, and by the time I'd reached it, I'd forgotten the previous twelve. I was starting to feel very cross with myself, and that reminded me of another story. When Saint David was very cross with himself, to say sorry to God, he would stand in a river, up to his neck in icy cold water, reciting scripture. I wonder if anyone sponsored him? I know someone who sat in a bath, up to their armpits in cold custard, singing 'Sosban Fach', and they raised £2,000 for *Children in Need.*

I decided to abandon the idea of learning every word in the dictionary on the grounds that I have a memory like a sieve (*cof fel rhidyll*). Instead, I decided to make a list of the most important words for making a Saint David's day picture out of ripped paper. *COCH* I wrote at the top in red pen. The colour of fiery Welsh dragons and the colour my face will turn

when I'm um-ing. I pictured ruby-red rugby shirts with grassy-green leeks pinned to them, and that's when I remembered how the leek became our national symbol.

One day Dewi was watching a furious fight between the Welsh and the Saxons. He had a sneaking feeling that the Welsh were losing, but it was a bit difficult to tell because everyone was dressed the same. They didn't have team colours and contrasting stripy socks in those days. Now I'm not sure if they were having their fight on Dewi's vegetable allotment, but apparently he scanned the ground around him, pulled up a leek, and quick as a flash shouted out, 'Welshmen, wear one of these on your helmet so that you'll recognise one another.' It's hard to imagine how they organised this. Someone must have called 'half time', because otherwise, as all the Welshmen bent down to pull up a leek, it would have been pretty easy for the Saxons to chop their heads off. Anyway, just imagine for a minute, the startling sight of an onslaught of soldiers with big smelly leeks flapping about on the front of their helmets. It did the trick. Thanks to Dewi, the Welsh won the battle.

Well this may come as a bit of a surprise to you, but just at that moment I started to relax and I made a decision. I decided that on *Dydd Gŵyl Dewi* I'm going to wear a red rugby shirt, a Welsh flag *sarong*, a tall black hat and the most enormous, magnificent leek I can find, fastened to the front of it. If the worst happens and the children of Abertwt can't hear my Welsh, they'll certainly be able to recognise my Welshness.

I'm off to make dinner now. I'm always hungry at the end of a busy day. Tomorrow, maybe I'll finish that list, and who knows, maybe we'll meet at your school one day.

Until then *diolch yn fawr*, you've been a great listener.

The Moving, Sighing Statue

Mary Medlicott

*Imagine a statue that moves.
Once a night, it lifts its right hand to turn over a page
of the book it is holding. You may not believe it, but I've
also been told this statue can sigh.*

Of course, if you heard it as you walked past, you might not pay any attention. You might think it was the sound of a breeze wafting by. But if you stopped and spoke to the statue, you could be in for a big surprise. You might even, if you waited, hear the statue speak back.

The statue I'm talking about is in a real place – you could go and see it right now if you wish – and the stories about it are not ancient and dusty. They're recent, which in a way makes it easier to believe them. Mind you, they come from children, and I know there are some strange people who don't believe a thing that children say – not their stories, anyway.

I disagree. Funny, sad, wonderful or weird, I think the stories children tell are usually well worth hearing.

With these particular stories, you must decide for yourself what to think. If you made up your mind to go and visit the statue, you could even collect your own evidence. The place to go is St Davids, which, as it happens, is a great place for a holiday. There are a lot of fine beaches and there's plenty to do. You could go out on a boat to visit the islands and see the seals and the puffins. You could go surfing. You could explore the coast path. And you should certainly go into St Davids Cathedral. To see the statue, however, you need to stay on the outside of the Cathedral.

If you get into the right position, you might even see the statue moving. As long as you go at midnight, of course. And best when the moon is full.

To locate the statue, go down the steps towards the Cathedral (you can count them, there are thirty-nine), then follow the pathway round to the right until you get to the West Door. This door is massive and hardly ever opened. Stand in front of it and then look up. Above the doorway, you'll see a stone statue of a monk who is holding a book. This is what you're looking for. According to local children, the statue is Saint David himself. At present, unfortunately, there's a kind of wire veil stretched across him. The wire is for a good reason – to keep the birds off. If you were a statue, you might prefer it to having a seagull perched on top of your head!

Fifty years ago, according to one of the statue stories, a Cathedral verger (that's a kind of caretaker) was living in a cottage the other side of the bridge just beyond the Cathedral. One night, this verger was clearing up before going to bed when he noticed there was a full moon. He went to take a look through his living-room window and, glancing towards the Cathedral, he noticed a movement high up on the wall above the great West Door. What he saw next made him jump.

He saw the statue lift its right arm and turn a page of its book.

In one respect, I'm sure you'll agree, this story makes a lot of sense: any person reading a book needs to turn over a page every now and again. The same must be true for a statue: it would be boring to stick on the same page for ever. Unfortunately, one other aspect of the story makes no sense at all. This is the bit about the verger's cottage. I have been to check it out. I have actually stood by the cottage window and I don't think anyone's got much chance of seeing the statue moving from there.

The verger's story is not the only one. Another which I've heard from children living in St Davids happened, they said, to a girl called Caroline. Caroline was in the choir at Ysgol Dewi Sant, the secondary school. One night, she had to take part in a Cathedral concert. Beforehand, she and her friends changed into their choir uniforms in a side-room towards the back of the church. The concert went on late (as school concerts often do) and at the end, they had to hurry to change and go home. Just as they were leaving, Caroline remembered her jumper. She'd left it in the changing room. 'Wait for me,' she said to her friends and quickly rushed to collect it. 'Typical,' she exclaimed when she reached the outside again. Her friends had gone. Caroline went towards the end of the building in case they were hiding round the corner, and as she got to the West Door, she heard a sound that caught her attention. It came from somewhere above her head. Caroline looked up and saw the statue lift its right arm and turn a page of its book.

The children who told me this story added that it was well past midnight when Caroline finally got home. They also told me there was a full moon that night.

Now when you think about these stories, you might conclude they were all made up – by local children. The children certainly seem to know a great deal about the statue man. Several times when I've asked what happens when he gets to the end of his book, they are quite definite about the answer. They say he closes the book, turns it over, then starts reading it again. They also seem to agree exactly how many pages there are in the book: 365. One for each day of the year. So far, I haven't found out what happens in a leap year!

About the statue man himself, the children have some different opinions. Some say he is made entirely of stone and that it's the stone that moves. Some say the stone is just a cover, and inside he's flesh and blood like us. Of course, the children of St Davids are not much different from children everywhere. They're lively and fun and they've got very good stories. But it may surprise you that there is one more story, one which doesn't come from St Davids. It was told to me in Bedford, in England, a long way away from St Davids. This is how the story goes.

A girl from Bedford – I was not given her name – was on holiday in St Davids with her parents. She could not get off to sleep on her first night, so her parents decided to take her for a walk in order to calm her down. They never imagined that that walk would have the opposite effect. Shortly before midnight they set out from the house they'd rented. It was a lovely moonlit night and first they walked down the little street called the Pebbles. Then they went through the great stone arch called the Bell Tower where the Cathedral bells are kept. Next, they climbed down the thirty-nine steps that lead down to the Cathedral. By the time they reached the Cathedral itself, the girl's parents were lagging behind. So she was on her own when she reached the great West Door. As she passed the doorway, she heard a very deep sigh. She looked round. There was no-one nearby. She heard the sound again and, this time, she knew for definite that it had come from above her head. She looked up and, miraculously, was just in time to see the statue man, with his right arm raised, turning a page of his book. He sighed again and looked very fed up. 'Is anything wrong?' the girl enquired.

'Yes,' the statue man replied. 'I'm bored with this book. I've been reading it for hundreds of years.'

Well, that night, the girl did not get a wink of sleep – and neither did her parents. By the morning, she'd decided what to do about the statue man's problem. She would have to get him a new book. But what book would it be and where would she get it? Fortunately, children can be very determined. By the time this girl from Bedford had finished her holiday, she'd managed to find a local stone carver and had paid him to create a new book for the statue. She'd also hired a crane, and on the last night of her holiday, she gave instructions as the crane was manouevred into position by the West Door of the Cathedral. The old book was changed for the new one and, when the old one was lifted down, it was hoisted into a van, which the girl had also hired, and then it was driven back to Bedford. There she kept it in her attic until, when she died as a very old lady, the book was brought down from the attic and used as the tombstone on her grave.

I cannot vouch for the truth of this story. All I know is that I found it well worth hearing. Not only was it told to me a long way away from St Davids, it was also, I thought, a very good story. It encourages me to end this report of mine about the moving, sighing statue with the hope that you, too, can go to St Davids. It's not only a wonderful place to spend a holiday; it's also a wonderful place to live. I know because, before I became a storyteller, visiting lots of children in schools, I grew up in St Davids myself.

Visiting Grandpa

Nicola Davies

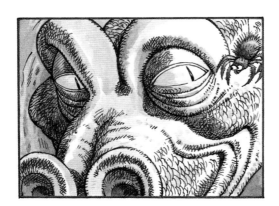

Most children love to visit their grandpa;
Delyth and Maldwyn had different ideas.

No-one wanted to visit Grandpa Noggard, not even his grandchildren.

'What's the point?' said Delyth. 'He's always sleeping in the darkest corner of his cave, with great hairy spiders crawling all over him. Sometimes, he even eats them!'

'When he snores,' added Maldwyn, 'he breathes out stinky green smoke.'

'No wonder your mother left him,' Mr Noggard told his wife.

'He still has some friends,' said Mrs Noggard.

'Has he?' said Mr Noggard. 'Who would that be? Your father's upset everyone. Gordo, the lake dragon, can't stand him; even Zogi the Invisible wants nothing to do with him.'

'But it's his birthday soon,' said Mrs Noggard. 'You'll come with us, won't you?'

'No way,' said her husband. 'He's *your* father. And anyway,' he added hastily, 'the cave door needs mending.'

'Very well,' said Mrs Noggard. 'I'll just take the children.'

Maldwyn and Delyth wailed, 'Do we have to visit Gramps? Can't we stay and help Dad?'

'You're coming and that's that,' said Mrs Noggard, firmly.

'What if Grandpa's asleep?'

'He always wakes up before Saint David's Day, in time for his birthday. He won't have eaten for five years; he'll be pleased to see you.'

'Why?' asked Maldwyn, innocently. 'Will he eat us?'

'Don't be silly,' said their mother. 'We're taking food, as usual. We'll set off before dawn, to avoid the humans.'

*   *   *

As dawn began to shrink shadows on the slopes of the Brecon Beacons, the dragons flew, hidden among the clouds. The dark slopes of the Beacons looked like frozen waves beneath them and the dragons could see the occasional lights of magical wheeled boxes.

The clouds whizzed across the sky, propelled by dragons' breath.

'I'm tired,' wailed Delyth. 'I'm getting out of puff.'

'We're nearly there,' said Mrs Noggard. 'Can't you see the smoke?'

Thick purply-green clouds met them at the mouth of Grandpa's cave.

'That's disgusting,' said Maldwyn, coughing.

'Follow me,' said Mrs Noggard, leading them through the oily smoke. In the furthest corner of the dark cave was Grandpa himself, covered in fly-spattered cobwebs; hairy black spiders hung from his nostrils.

'Gross,' said Maldwyn, coughing and spluttering.

'He's not moved an inch since last time,' said Delyth.

'He'll wake any minute,' said their mother. 'Delyth, blow Grandpa's cobwebs away while we get the food ready.' She started unloading fruit onto Grandpa's rock table: ten hands of bananas, a hundred oranges, an apple tree.

Delyth squatted in front of Grandpa, blowing away the thick cobwebs, watching hairy spiders scuttling into deep rock crevices. Suddenly, she saw a massive eyelid quiver. The eye opened, fixing its watery red pupil on hers. Grandpa scratched a dead spider from his nose and yawned purple flames. Delyth jumped back: Grandpa was awesome.

'Had a good rest, Dad?' asked their mother. 'Feeling peckish?'

'Who are you?' said Grandpa.

'Not that again,' said Mrs Noggard. 'You're always like this after a sleep. You'll feel better with some nice green bananas inside you.'

Grandpa took two lumbering steps to reach the rock table. He sucked, and several hands of bananas flew into his massive mouth, peel and all.

'That's not fair,' said Maldwyn. 'You might have left us some.'

'Have an apple,' boomed Grandpa, holding the tree steady for Delyth and Maldwyn. He took a large bite of tree, then another . . . and it was gone.

Maldwyn was impressed. 'You'll have stomach-ache, Grandpa.'

'Now, Dad,' said Mrs Noggard, 'what do you want for your birthday next week?'

Grandpa Noggard emitted a long banana belch. 'I want . . . to be left alone.'

'Don't be such a grump,' she said. 'It's your 1,500th birthday. I'm making fruity-vegetable cake with cabbage, strawberries, sprouts, bananas, turnips and red ants.'

'Delicious,' said Grandpa. 'Who's coming to share it? I hope you didn't invite the lake dragon . . . we're not on speaking terms.'

'Not to worry,' said his daughter. 'He's not coming.'

'Oh.' Grandpa sounded disappointed. 'And Zogi the Invisible?' He saw his daughter's expression. 'He's not coming either?'

There was a long silence.

'Then who *is* coming?' whispered Grandpa.

'Well,' said Mrs Noggard at last, 'I'll be there. And the children.'

Grandpa lumbered out of his cave and sat at the entrance.

'Poor Grandpa,' said Delyth.

'It's his own fault,' said Maldwyn. 'He's quarrelled with everyone, including Dad.'

'I know,' said Delyth. 'Maybe he still misses Grandma. It's only 500 years since she left him and it is his birthday next week. Look at him. He's so unhappy. We'll have to do something.'

Grandpa was still sitting on the rocky ledge when they set off for home. It looked like he was part of the rock itself.

* * *

That night, when their parents were asleep, the children set off to the home of the lake dragon: Llangors. It was midnight when they landed and saw the lake shining like a fallen star.

66

Maldwyn stepped towards some dark humps on the footpath, then jumped back as a peeved swan hissed at him.

'Where *is* the dragon?' asked Delyth, staring across the shining expanse of water. 'There's no sign of him.'

Suddenly, the surface of the water lifted up like a lid and a huge water dragon emerged, tall as a rowan, transparent as ice. The splendid creature was fashioned from running water. In the moonlight, his teeth flashed like silver icicles.

'Children,' he said in a crystal voice, 'what can I do for you?'

'We've come to invite you to Grandpa Noggard's birthday.'

Small fountains of water spurted everywhere as the lake dragon laughed. 'Has he put you up to this? Does he want to make friends at last?'

Delyth looked into the sparkling eyes of the lake dragon and had to tell the truth. 'No, he doesn't. But it is his 1,500th birthday on Saint David's Day. No-one's coming. Just us.'

Bubbles of water rippled across the lake dragon's face. 'Your grandfather's upset everyone, hasn't he? He wasn't always like that. We used to have picnics here, in Saint David's time. Your grandfather, Saint David and me.'

'You knew Saint David?'

'Of course. He often used to walk in this lake. *Dewi Dyfrwr*, we called him.' The lake dragon's eyes glittered in the moonlight. 'Nothing like old times. All right, children, I'll come . . . for old times' sake.'

'You won't be upset if Grandpa ignores you?'

'Why should I?' said the lake dragon. 'He hasn't spoken to me for over 500 years, as it is.'

The lake birds were stirring. Swans and geese raised their heads to greet the early morning light. 'Humans will be arriving soon,' said the lake dragon. 'Was there anything else?'

'We were wondering about inviting other dragons,' said Delyth.

'Where could we find Zogi the Invisible?' said Maldwyn.

'Leave it with me,' said the lake dragon. 'I'll tell him.'

As they flew home, well-pleased with their night's work, Maldwyn said, 'If Zogi's invisible . . . how will we be able to tell even if he does come to the party?'

*   *   *

It was Saint David's Day . . . Grandpa's birthday. He sat on the rocky ledge in the rain, sulking. Mrs Noggard and the children were inside, hanging up the party decorations: banana peel and bunches of cabbage leaves.

'Is Grandpa going to stay like that all day?' asked Delyth.

'If he doesn't move soon,' said their mother, grimly, 'we're going home.' She went out to her father. 'Dad, you're spoiling things for your grandchildren, as well as yourself.'

Grandpa stared silently at the unyielding Beacons slopes.

Suddenly a swarm of raindrops appeared, merging to form the lake dragon. He looked even larger by day. 'I've brought guests with me,' he said.

No time to ask who they were: a voice cut through the air.

'You miserable old goboletch,' it shouted. 'Stop being sorry for yourself . . . now!'

'It's the wife!' said Grandpa Noggard, racing into his cave.

'Mother,' said Mrs Noggard, 'where *have* you been?'

'Travelling,' said Grandma Noggard. 'Didn't you get my messages? Are these my lovely grandchildren?' Without waiting for an answer, she dashed after her husband.

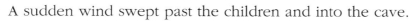

A sudden wind swept past the children and into the cave.

'That'll be Zogi the Invisible,' said Maldwyn, knowingly.

'True,' said a voice, as the children's father stepped down from a nearby cloud.

'Dad. You came.'

'I couldn't miss the fun, could I?' said Mr Noggard.

It wasn't long before Grandpa and Grandma Noggard were throwing fruit and vegetables at each other. 'You stupid finkleweed,' she said, aiming a turnip at him.

'Who told you to go gallivanting?' he said, responding with a purple cabbage.

Mr Noggard helped himself to a slice of vegetable cake. 'Come on, everyone,' he said. 'Eat now, before they throw all the food at each other.'

Maldwyn grabbed some bananas and handed one to Delyth. They ducked as a purple parsnip hit the cave wall. Then Grandpa flew past, followed by Grandma shouting, 'Come back, you old lambickle.'

'He's getting some exercise at last,' said Mrs Noggard, happily.

'Come outside, everyone,' said the lake dragon. 'This is going to be a 1,500th birthday party to remember! Pity Saint David himself couldn't be here. It's his day too, after all.'

Saint David's Day

Lisa Daniels

Dressed up in *pais a betgwn*
Of red Welsh flannel,
A woollen shawl
And a black hat over a frilled bonnet,
A bright yellow daffodil
Pinned carefully on my shawl,
Proudly, I walk to school.

Listening to tales of old –
The ground rising at Llanddewi Brefi,
Blind Paulinus' sight restored,
The monastery at Glyn Rhosyn
On the banks of the small river Alun –
We lunch on cawl and buttery Welsh cakes.

Dressed in *pais a betgwn*

We make our way home,

Daffodils and leeks withered.

Hats and bonnets swing from hands.

We are all joyful.

We shall do the little things:

Dewi would be proud of us today.

Note: in traditional Welsh costume, the *betgwn* is an open-fronted gown worn over the *pais*, a petticoat made from flannel.

The Boat

Christine Evans

There were already seven of them,
three boys growing like weeds and four girls
forever squabbling for space, so when
Gwyn's mam found herself getting big again,
she was at her wits' end.

'This cottage is too small!' they heard her telling their father. 'Where am I to put the new baby when it comes? There's five of them on that mattress in the loft, and Nain in the box bed by the fire – and the twins still in with us. No room to swing a cat in here! And what'll I do with wet clothes all through the winter?'

The boys were helping their father plait leather strips into a rope. They kept their heads down, working at the knots. Rain poured down outside, bouncing on the stones and running into muddy streams.

'Well – Annie and Mari are getting big enough to help in the house, and watch the little ones while you do the milking and the washing – and

Gwilym's really good at weeding turnips. Perhaps I should make a bed for the boys in the barn with the old cow and the dog – they'll be all right if we gather plenty of bracken, once it's dry.'

'And what am I to feed them all on, then?'

Gareth pinched Gwyn but he didn't even squeak. He knew better than to catch his mother's eye, but she'd seen him wince as she turned from the fire.

'*He's* not much use for anything. Except scrounging for something to eat.' Tiredness and worry had made her voice hard. 'Look how small and skinny he is. After his birthday, he'd better go to work for the monks; they're always ready to take healthy boys once they're ten.'

His father was quiet for a moment, then he grunted as if he'd made up his mind. 'And they might teach him the letters. He might have a chance to learn writing.'

'Fat lot of good that would be!' She slapped the bread dough hard on the table. 'There's no call for that in this village. It'll just be one less mouth to feed.'

So here he was, six months later, walking the beaches of the little Island in the Currents, or as some called it, the Island of the Brothers. It was a bright, breezy day at the end of winter, the seagulls dancing high above and seals on the rocks calling to each other. Later, there would be a special service and a feast, because it was the day to remember Saint David, who had travelled across the world to Jerusalem. Gwyn did a little dance of pleasure at not being cooped up in the smoky scriptorium, struggling to copy the words of the Bible, all those meaningless black marks wriggling like tadpoles and making his eyes hurt. Other boys seemed to see sense in them, but he just couldn't. He got by because he could remember the stories, and most of the hymns and the prayers: once he'd heard something twice, it stuck in his head. The choirmaster didn't think much of his voice either, though he sang as loudly as any, and chanted joyfully in Latin.

He stretched his arms out, enjoying the feeling of being strong. For the first winter in his life, there had been enough to eat – thick porridge every morning, stew and oatcakes and a bit of cheese for dinner, and a hot milk posset at day's end. Gwyn had soon grown out of the clothes he had come in. Now he wore a tunic of thick wool from the island's own sheep, and strong leather sandals so he could run across the sharp rocks without hurting his feet.

He'd been sad and scared at first, leaving his home and his family, but from the first moment he stepped into the rocking boat, he had loved the sea. He would have liked to work on the boat, crossing backwards and forwards to the mainland to bring visitors and supplies, but only the strongest and most skilled of the brothers could do that. As often as he could, he escaped from weeding vegetables or skipped lessons to run down to the shore. The waves brought all sorts of useful things, and it was fun finding them. On an island where the wind was too strong and salty for trees to grow, driftwood for the fire often saved him from a scolding. A good leather flask, still half-full of sweet water, earned him a pat on the head from Father Abbot himself, who told him it would be kept for the next brother called to journey across the ocean to preach the word of

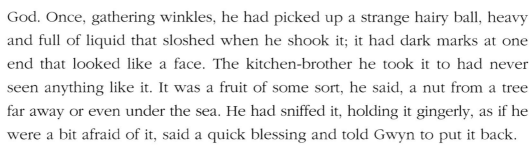

God. Once, gathering winkles, he had picked up a strange hairy ball, heavy and full of liquid that sloshed when he shook it; it had dark marks at one end that looked like a face. The kitchen-brother he took it to had never seen anything like it. It was a fruit of some sort, he said, a nut from a tree far away or even under the sea. He had sniffed it, holding it gingerly, as if he were a bit afraid of it, said a quick blessing and told Gwyn to put it back.

The boy had hoped it was something tasty they could eat. In wintertime there wasn't much fresh food: everyone was fed up with salted herring. One day he found a pool in a hidden, narrow gully where a long silver fish had got trapped when the tide went out. Soon after, there was a big crab half-out of the water. It was quite a job to catch hold of it without getting nipped by its big claws, but he managed it and this time Brother Elfed was so pleased he made it Gwyn's job to walk all round the island every day to see what he could bring back. Now he wouldn't have to trudge for hours behind the plough, picking up stones, or get bored herding the goats or cleaning out the pigs. He had his own, special work.

But his luck seemed to have run out. For days the pool was empty, until he thought of moving some of the stones to make a channel leading to the sea, where three or four seals were always watching. As he worked to build his fish-trap, his foot slipped on the seaweedy rocks and suddenly he was in deep water, sinking down. After the first shock though, his legs started to move and his arms to flap like wings. He found he could keep afloat and splash back to land, spluttering and coughing, but not afraid. He could swim like the seals!

And his fish-trap worked. The brothers thanked God for sending the fish that Gwyn took to the cook often now, and he could get away to the beach every day after morning prayers. Today, gulls had printed the wet sand with patterns, each webbed foot making a mark like a tiny house roof, and for a moment he thought of his family, and wondered how Nain was after the winter and if Mari's cough was worse. He missed his sisters most.

He thought of walking into the house and saying, 'Look, I'm not skinny any more and I'm certainly not useless.' But then the bright sea winking at him and the seals' singing called him back, and he scampered along the beach. Round the rocks at the end, the sea filled the gully like a small harbour, with a whole crowd of black heads bobbing in smooth water, all looking at him with big, dark, curious eyes. Then the seals dived, all at once, leaving only splashes, as if he'd thrown a handful of stones . . . but there was something left, a long dark shape floating, just under the surface.

At first he thought it was a seal, sleeping or dead, but as he clambered nearer he could see it was a big tree trunk. He stripped off his tunic, untied the thongs of his sandals and waded in. The cold sea took his breath away, but he reached the log and pulled it up on the sand. Water drained out of it as he turned it over: it was hollowed out; he could see the knife marks where somebody had carved a place to sit. It was a boat!

He was wet already, so he climbed into the boat and sat down. It was hard and not very comfortable, but the fit was just right. He looked out across the miles of sea, wondering where it could have come from. A place where trees grew strong, away from the sea, that was for sure. Sometimes after sunset, mountains could be seen far away on the horizon and the brothers told stories of a green land with many lakes and rivers. Some of them had travelled there. A country miles away where people made boats differently, ate different food, talked a strange language.

A little gust of wind lifted his hair and he tasted salt on his lips. He imagined pulling the boat into the water, jumping in – he'd have to make a paddle like the brothers used in the coracles – and pushing off. He thought of how the log would lift to the first wave, stirring under him as though it were coming alive again.

He smiled, opening his face to the sun's warmth and the shining sky. Now he would be able to go fishing properly, with a line or a net. He faced out towards the open sea, the horizons, other beaches beckoning.

Castle Nevermore

Ruth Morgan

Characters

Narrator 1

Narrator 2

Gethin – a young traveller

Betsan – An old woman

A Guard

A Cook

A Doctor

The Lord Pedr

Mair – a young Victorian girl

Tegid – a Wizard

SCENE 1: ON THE HILLSIDE

NARRATOR 1: One bright Saint David's Day morning, a young lad named Gethin was strolling in the hills in the middle of Wales. He climbed onto a large stone, the better to enjoy the beautiful view. All of a sudden, a mighty rumble shook the ground beneath the stone.

Sound effect: a loud rumble, like thunder.

GETHIN: What in the name of Welsh cakes was that?

Sound effect: an enormous rush of wind.

NARRATOR 2: Then poor Gethin was thrown into the air by a torrent of wind which blasted from the earth. It catapulted the stone just as though it were the stopper in a bottle of fizzy pop. When Gethin landed, he was in deep shadow.

GETHIN: Help! What's happening?

NARRATOR 1: Gethin staggered to his feet only to find himself standing in the courtyard of a mighty castle, its high walls capped by towers and turrets.

NARRATOR 2: The floor of the courtyard was covered in snow. The air was icy cold, even though Gethin could still see the warm blue sky smiling overhead.

GETHIN: Brrr! It's f . . . f . . . f . . . freezing in here.

Enter an old woman, carrying a bundle of sticks. Gethin doesn't see her yet.

GETHIN: What is this place? Am I dreaming? Maybe I hit my head when I fell.

The Old Woman drops her bundle in surprise.

OLD WOMAN: Who are you? Has the Wizard Llwyd sent you? Have you come to help us, or . . . or . . ?

The old woman shrieks and runs away, waving her arms wildly above her head.

GETHIN: Come back! That was weird. Why was she so scared of me? Well, I'm not hanging around where I'm not wanted. I'm off!

Gethin walks over to the open gateway. As he does so, the portcullis begins to lower.

GETHIN: Hey!

As Gethin arrives at the gateway, the portcullis clangs shut against the ground. He beats at the portcullis with his hands.

GETHIN: Ow! It's made of ice!

Gethin places one finger on the portcullis, then pulls it away sharply and sucks it.

GETHIN: Ice frozen so hard it burns!

Enter the Old Woman, a Guard, a Cook and a Doctor, all dressed in medieval clothes.

OLD WOMAN: That's him! He came from nowhere. Llwyd must have sent him.

GUARD:	Right, you. Tell us, have you come to help us solve the puzzle?
COOK:	Please say you've come to free us from this prison.
GETHIN:	I don't know what you're talking about!
GUARD:	Llwyd hasn't sent you?
GETHIN:	I don't know any Llwyd. Now, pull up that portcullis and let me go!
DOCTOR:	You really don't know where you are?
GETHIN:	I swear! One minute I'm standing enjoying the view; the next I'm flying through the air, then I land in this dreadful place.
DOCTOR:	Then heaven help you, you poor lad. You'd better come with us.

Exit Gethin and the courtiers

SCENE 2: THE GREAT HALL

The Lord Pedr is sitting on his throne, surrounded by sombre-looking courtiers including the Old Woman, Guard, Cook and Doctor. Gethin stands before them. To one side of the throne is an ornate wooden chest.

DOCTOR:	Your Lordship, he swears he is not from Llwyd and I believe him.
LORD PEDR:	Indeed?

GETHIN: Will someone tell me how I can get out of here?

LORD PEDR: Well, if we could tell you that, we wouldn't be here
                 ourselves.

GETHIN: What do you mean?

LORD PEDR: *[ignoring Gethin]* Betsan, have you stacked the firewood at
                 the gate?

OLD WOMAN: I have, My Lord.

DOCTOR: Although I don't see . . .

LORD PEDR: *[shouting]* What? What don't you see?

DOCTOR: We try to melt the portcullis each year. It never
                 works. The hotter the fire gets, the more the
                 ice seems to thicken.

LORD PEDR: Well, when you come up with a better idea,
                 just let me know, you scoundrel. We'll light the
                 fire as usual.

GETHIN: Excuse me . . .

LORD PEDR: Silence, you!

COOK: What about the chest, My Lord?

LORD PEDR: Tegid has come up with a new spell, but we need to be out
                 in the open air. Come, there's no time to waste. Guard,
                 bring the chest.

                 *Exit the Lord Pedr, followed by the Guard carrying
                 the chest, and the other courtiers. The only ones left*

*in the Hall are Gethin and a girl called Mair who is
dressed in Victorian clothes.*

MAIR: It happened to me, too.

GETHIN: You mean . . .

MAIR: It was Saint David's Day, 1897. I was
           out for a walk and, like you, became
           imprisoned here. My name is Mair.

GETHIN: But what is this place?

MAIR: Castle Nevermore. It only exists on
           one day a year, the first of March. So
           we creep inch by inch through our
           lives, living one day each year,
           miserable in the knowledge that
           there's no escape.

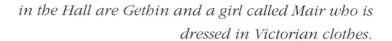

GETHIN: Where are you the rest of the year?

Mair simply points at the ground and pulls a grim face.

GETHIN: But that's horrific! How did it all happen? And why is there
           no escape?

MAIR: Pedr is a cruel Lord, and a foolish one. He made the
           mistake of trying to double-cross a powerful Wizard.

GETHIN: Llwyd?

MAIR: That's right. Llwyd accused Pedr of not valuing the most
           important things in life. He said he would turn this castle
           into a reflection of Pedr's mean soul.

GETHIN: A frozen prison . . .

MAIR: But he left a puzzle, a single way out. If someone can only solve it, the spell will break and we shall all be free.

GETHIN: What is it?

MAIR: If anyone can turn whatever is in that chest to gold, the icy portcullis will melt. The trouble is, no-one knows how to do it. Pedr's own Wizard, Tegid, is always trying . . . and failing.

GETHIN: So what's in the chest?

MAIR: I don't know.

GETHIN: Well, I have to know. Come on, which way were they going?

MAIR: Outside. Believe me: they can't have gone far.

Exit Gethin and Mair.

SCENE 3: THE COURTYARD

Lord Pedr and his courtiers are gathered around the closed chest.
Gethin rushes into the courtyard, followed by Mair.

GETHIN: I must see what's in the chest.

LORD PEDR: Seize him!

The Guard steps forward and pins Gethin's arms behind his back.

LORD PEDR: The fire has been lit?

OLD WOMAN: Yes, although it doesn't seem to be making much difference. The ice seems thicker than ever.

LORD PEDR: Where is that fool Tegid? Time's running out.

Enter Tegid

TEGID: Here I am, My Lord.

LORD PEDR: This new spell of yours, it had better work.

TEGID: I'm confident it'll work this time. I'll turn the contents of the chest to precious gold before your very eyes.

LORD PEDR: Just get on with it!

The Guard and Cook step forward and open the lid of the chest. Tegid circles the chest three times, dropping pinches of powder into the chest as he chants.

TEGID: *[chanting]* Turn, turn to glittering gold,
That all of us may here behold.
This Saint David's Day we'll see
Pedr rescued, rich and free!

Lord Pedr and the courtiers creep forward to peer inside the chest.

LORD PEDR: *[angrily]* It's made no difference! You'll pay for this, Tegid.

The courtiers groan. Gethin manages to struggle free of the Guard and pushes through the crowd.

GETHIN: Let me see what's in there!

Gethin grabs one side of the chest and the Cook grabs the other. There is a struggle, which ends in a pile of daffodil bulbs spilling out onto the floor.

TEGID: Stop him!

Gethin picks up a bulb.

GETHIN: But I know what to do! I know how to change these into gold!

DOCTOR: Then show us, lad.

Gethin kneels and begins planting the bulbs in the earth, digging with his hands.

TEGID: My Lord, this is madness!

GETHIN: But if I'm right, and the Wizard gave you magic bulbs . . .

Sound effect: magical 'growing' music. Golden daffodils appear from the earth. The courtiers gasp.

MAIR: Beautiful golden daffodils!

GETHIN: But of course you were expecting the other kind of gold, Pedr.

The Old Woman points in the direction of the gates.

OLD WOMAN: Look! The portcullis has melted! We're free!

*All the courtiers rush to the gates and exit.
The only ones left are Lord Pedr, Gethin and Mair.*

LORD PEDR: *[shouting]* Come back, I command you. You'll only leave when I say so. I'm still your Lord and Master.

MAIR: It's too late. They've gone.

GETHIN: And nowadays, there aren't any Lords ruling the castles. You're out of a job, Pedr. There's no-one left for you to bully. It seems that the Wizard Llwyd has had his perfect revenge.

*Exit Lord Pedr,
his head bowed.*

MAIR: I'm scared. I don't know anything about your world.

GETHIN: Well, it's a place where we still celebrate Saint David's Day. Come with me and I'll show you!

Exit Gethin and Mair.

NARRATOR 1: Gethin and Mair stepped out onto a bright hillside where every dancing daffodil seemed to promise a golden future.

NARRATOR 2: And as for Castle Nevermore . . . it was never seen again.

Dragons and Daffodils

Neil Nuttall

You wouldn't catch me holding
a dragon these days but back then
I couldn't have been more proud.
It was a Friday and Dad was waiting
for us when we came out of school.
I couldn't wait to show him what I'd
made for Saint David's Day.

'Wow, Sioned, what a fantastic dragon!'

Then Ieuan arrived and showed Dad his daffodils. 'They're red,' said Ieuan. 'Only the Juniors were allowed to make dragons. All the Infants had to make daffodils. I didn't want to make a vase of silly yellow daffodils. I wanted to make a red dragon. Miss made me stay in until I'd painted my daffodils so I painted them red like a dragon. She was a bit cross but not much. I was the only one with red daffodils.'

When we got home, we had tea, with the dragon and the daffodils on the table. Mum said they were both brilliant – though it was the first time she'd seen red daffodils. Dad was acting funny – daydreaming with a silly grin on his face.

Ieuan and I helped Mum clear the table while Dad sat twirling one of the red daffodils. 'I'd forgotten,' he said. 'Fancy me forgetting something like that.'

Mum said that she hoped he wasn't going to forget about the washing up too! Dad chased her round the table with my dragon until she collapsed laughing on the sofa. 'I've told Sioned and Ieu to take their models to Nain's tomorrow,' he said. 'I think she'll be really pleased to see them.'

Ieuan and I love going to visit Nain Price. Not just for the *losin*, the sweets she keeps in a battered *Quality Street* tin, but mostly because although she's a grown up, she behaves like one of us. She can skip better than me and flick elastic bands further than Ieu!

Mum and Dad were all excited about their trip to Cardiff when they dropped us off at Nain's house. She told us to put the dragon and the daffodils on the kitchen table next to a big vase of real daffodils. Ieuan told Nain about what happened in school and how his were probably the only red daffodils ever in the whole world. Nain chuckled and said that she wasn't so sure about that.

Then Ieu caught sight of Nain's wheelbarrow outside the backdoor. 'Rides!' he shouted. He leapt into the barrow and sat with his legs dangling between the handles, waiting for Nain. I lifted one handle and Nain the other. We set off at a gallop across the grass, the barrow wiggling almost as much as the path did.

When we got to the edge of the lawn, Nain slowed down and carefully steered the barrow along the path to the old shed. 'Out you jump,' she said to Ieuan. 'We need to load up with tools for our jobs.'

Ieuan and I said, 'What jobs?'

'As it's such a lovely day, I thought we might give the garden a spring-clean.' She handed me a rake, gave Ieuan an old bucket, put a pair of grass-clippers in the wheelbarrow and cried, 'Follow me!'

We began under the fruit trees. Nain clipped and pulled out dead grass. I raked out the leaves and Ieuan collected them and made piles by the path. It didn't seem long before Nain stopped and said, 'Time for a break!'

As she went back to the house to collect the elevenses, Ieuan and I had a look to see what was different since our last visit. Peeping out from behind one of the apple trees were three tiny daffodils. Nain appeared, balancing mugs, a plate of biscuits and the *losin* tin on a tray above her head. 'Taraa . . !' she said and plonked the tray next to us.

When we'd finished our drinks and biscuits, Nain opened the sweet tin. 'Look what I've found!' she said. '*Losin!*' From the tin she lifted three hard round sugary sweets.

I knew what they were, 'Extra hot mint imperials!' I said. I don't like them if I'm honest, but I didn't want to hurt Nain's feelings. 'Not for me just at the moment,' I said.

Ieuan was a lot less polite. 'I hate those,' he said, pulling a face.

But Nain picked the mints up, rubbed them in her hands and . . . talked to them! 'That's where you went,' she said. She twinkled her eyes and said that if I didn't want one, and Ieuan didn't like them, we should ask the little daffodils if they'd like one. I ask you, which one of us is the grown-up? Even Ieuan lost his sulk and told Nain that flowers don't eat sweets.

'These might, if we ask them nicely,' chuckled Nain and she made us put our faces level with the daffodils. She showed Ieu how to pop the mints into their trumpets. Daft daffodils! I looked up at the sky and watched the clouds chase each other. Nain and Ieu stopped talking and I shut my eyes.

Schlooock . . . schloop . . .

It sounded as though someone, or something, was sucking.

'Sion! Look!'

I opened my eyes; Nain and Ieuan were still gazing at the daffodils – red daffodils!

I closed my eyes, opened them and looked at the daffodils again. They were still red. I rubbed my eyes.

Ieuan scrabbled in the tin for a fresh supply of mints. 'You do it, Sion! You do it like I did,' he pleaded.

I looked at Nain; she raised her eyebrows and nodded. We bent down and I carefully popped one hot mint into each red daffodil trumpet. 'Close your eyes and listen,' said Nain. Ieuan and I bent down.

Schlooock . . . schloop . . .

Somebodies or somethings were sucking again. My nose started to twitch. I was sure that I could smell smoke. I heard Ieuan sniff and sneeze as Nain told us to open our eyes.

'What are those?' asked Ieuan. 'They still look like my red daffodils, but . . .'

'They're a bit like dragons as well,' I said.

I looked and looked again. The red daffodils still had their petals, but now they had tiny eyes. And not only eyes, but tiny teeth and tiny tongues too. Smoke curled from tiny nostrils. They were daffodils and dragons at the same time.

'I know what you are,' Ieuan said. 'You're *daffagons*!'

Nain said what a clever boy he was, just like our dad had been. I looked at her and she winked. Then it was her turn to feed the daffagons. This time Ieuan and I watched as Nain carefully gave each daffagon a mint. We saw them begin to suck, heard the *schlooock . . . schloop . . .* and watched as they turned into three tiny red dragons! They sat on the grass, their tails tightly curled around each other so it was difficult to see where one dragon ended and the next began.

We soon discovered that having three tiny dragons in the garden was fun. They followed us like puppies, tripping over their tails and lying on their backs to have their tummies tickled. Ieu threw a stick and they played chase and fetch. I threw a stick that went looping in the air and they discovered their wings. One flew up and sat on Nain's shoulder, blowing smoke rings above her head.

The rest of the day was like a dream. Nain kept tidying and we helped where we could. The dragons helped too, setting fire to the piles of weeds and dead leaves that Ieuan made. Best of all were the tick and chase games. Ieuan sulked when the dragons perched on the branches so he couldn't reach them. Nain put him in the wheelbarrow and pushed him round the garden to chase away his mood. The dragons flew down and balanced cheekily on the edge of the barrow. Ieuan leapt out at once and we all gave the dragons a turn round the garden, whizzing them in and out of the trees until we were out of breath. Then we played hide and seek.

After a while I saw that Nain had started to gather up the tools and wheel them back to the shed. 'Mum and Dad will be here soon,' she said.

'We can show them the dragons,' said Ieuan, looking round to see where they had gone. We couldn't see them at first. Ieuan found them. They were huddling together under the apple trees. Their tails were wound tightly around each other and wisps of smoke drifted into the cool afternoon air.

Suddenly Ieuan thought he heard the sound of a car and ran towards the house. Nain leaned against the apple tree and smiled at the dragons. I cwtshed up next to her. I heard the car stop and the doors open.

I looked across at Nain. Together we looked back at the dragons. Suddenly they didn't seem so fiery any more. Stiffer somehow, their wings looked more like petals and the curling smoke just wasn't there.

By the time Ieuan came running back across the grass, Nain and I had watched the dragons fade back into daffagons and red daffodils and finally . . .

Ieuan arrived just as the last daffodil was turning from red to orange to yellow. His face fell. 'Oh, Nain, they've gone. I wanted to show Mum and Dad.'

Nain picked him up and whispered something in his ear. Then she winked at me and said that we should tell Mum about the daffagons.

'But I think,' she said, looking over at Dad, 'your father already knows all about them!'

A gift for
St David's Day

ANSWER TO THE QUESTION ON PAGE 33

Francesca Kay writes:

In the second line of each verse I've used the word 'spring', and said something about it. In the third line each time I've written about the seasons changing. Perhaps you could try a poem with a similar pattern, or perhaps you can think of a different pattern of your own.
